What Girls Learn

poems by

Anne Dyer Stuart

Finishing Line Press
Georgetown, Kentucky

What Girls Learn

Copyright © 2021 by Anne Dyer Stuart
ISBN 978-1-64662-715-8 First Edition
All rights reserved under International and Pan-American Copyright Conventions. No part of this book may be reproduced in any manner whatsoever without written permission from the publisher, except in the case of brief quotations embodied in critical articles and reviews.

ACKNOWLEDGMENTS

"Marital Congress." *Cherry Tree*
"Inheritance." *AGNI*, 2016 Nominated for Best New Poets
"The Levee." *Louisiana Literature*
"Oxbow Lake." *Sugar House Review*
"Tiny" and "[summer snuck into fall again]." *The Louisville Review*
"What Girls Learn." *North Dakota Quarterly*
"Quick Magic." *Pembroke Magazine*
"Playboy." *Raleigh Review*
"Put Yourself Out There." *Exit 7*
"You Can't Outrun the Girl Inside Your Head." *Pembroke Magazine*
"First Grade." *storySouth*
"Mute." *Manor House Quarterly*
"Scars." *r.kv.r.y. quarterly literary journal*
"Ruined Ghazal." *Midway Journal*

Publisher: Leah Huete de Maines
Editor: Christen Kincaid
Cover Art: Claude Stuart
Author Photo: Anne Dyer Stuart
Cover Design: Elizabeth Maines McCleavy

Order online: www.finishinglinepress.com
also available on amazon.com

Author inquiries and mail orders:
Finishing Line Press
PO Box 1626
Georgetown, Kentucky 40324
USA

Table of Contents

Marital Congress 1

Inheritance 2

The Levee 3

Oxbow Lake 4

Tiny 5

[summer snuck into fall again] 6

What Girls Learn 7

Quick Magic 8

Playboy 9

Put Yourself Out There 10

You Can't Outrun the Girl Inside Your Head 12

First Grade 13

Mute 14

Scars 15

Ruined Ghazal 16

Wanted 17

In the Fog 18

Dirty Laundry 19

Practice 20

The Note 22

Still April and No Spring 23

Temporary 24

In the Classroom Is a Body 26

Odes in Juvenile Prison 27

All We Know 28

Limits 29

Marital Congress

Marital congress, Mama
says to me over the phone. *Baby,
it's too important.*

   Congress: a coming together, a meeting, an opposition, attraction, repulsion.
        A body, a settlement, a body elected, the session
        of this body.
        This body is in session.

   Regress: returning home as an adult.
    To exhibit retrograde motion. Or no motion at all. Poured over
        the red couch like syrup
        from a toddler's hands.

        To withdraw from the land. To return to subjects
        people thought were done.
                To atrophy, to degenerate, shrink.
                To disappear.

Whole opera of childhood,
operation on the body. Body
in childhood. Body
left behind.

        We are all of us little sacks of grief. Do not pretend
        otherwise. In the night
                with its wide open mouth, so black teeth hide
                behind its roar.

This is no way to be understood.

Each time we remember
we change the story.

Inheritance

I came here muscled like a foal,
rippled in winter sunlight, pale. Eyes
black holes into which everything fell,
and here was a land of giants, footprints
big as dinosaurs', some bland family resemblance.
Hunger in the stomach like a stone.
I came here wanting to be seen and then,
just as quick, invisible. Tiny
girls and their Delta mamas,
cottage cheese lunches, starched napkins,
inherited silver.
I came here from a long line of women who danced
with purses when the men pooped out.
I came here, daughter
to Miss Hospitality 1968, daughter
to worry, daughter to breast implants
and Revlon's Fire and Ice,
pantyhose in Easter egg containers
and Oriental rugs made new
with magic marker.
I came here wanting to be wanted,
to disappear, to blaze up
like a prom dress thrown on a campfire.
I came here, no debutante,
no dream imagined,
no daughter with a daughter
to try again,
to find herself on new soil
with the same destination.
A terrible beauty, this earth,
sandy loam, cotton fields
like parts in a girl's head.
Death unexpected in all things:
death here, too.

The Levee

Her best friend, best friend to everyone, gets out of the car at the stop sign, opens the driver's door and crawls in a boy's lap behind the wheel, a once-white cast on her arm now gray and covered in signatures. Down the block her parents are out of town and her little brother's on the roof preparing to jump into the neighbor's pool. She's about to be shipped a thousand miles away to boarding school, so she runs, tries to stretch her body lean at four feet nine. Boys throw fireworks as they move up and down the levee on the Fourth of July, her friend back in the passenger seat, giggling. Delta air so thick it's solid. She's going to Connecticut. First, Daddy will send her to field hockey and lacrosse camp, two sports she's never played because they don't exist here. Below the levee her older brother's on Lake Ferguson in a speed boat cracking open another Natural Light, that ass of a boy she used to date and his brother scouting girls, not paying attention to the barge and what it will mean to her brother on skis. There are a hundred ways to make yourself over, to stare at the water until you stare at yourself, until you see only yourself, determined to know what it is to know, determined.

Oxbow Lake

Front page of the paper, penciled
-in eyebrows in pixilated grain, collapsed
on the sidewalk in a paper jumpsuit,
gangbraids tight to her head.
"I was asleep," she said.
No girl, you were cooking meth
in a Victorian with turrets
and deep summer porches.
Neighbors applaud your arrest,
mutter words like *deserve*. That boy
next to you, crumples
in vindication, mouth like a scar.
Upstairs: a little girl barely four
in an Old Navy sweatshirt
and pink Keds.
Grudges held in the body
are held in the body now.
Focus: this river is trapped
by that levee and here
is where the world stops being round.
You can drop off, a knife edge,
you can disappear.

Tiny

the subject of this poem is tiny: high
school and all its horrors

spied with tiny eyes out-
side a tiny mind

down the hall of the macabre
enter and shrink

like a worm in sun
leather finger on the lawn

pawned by a bird and its dead
black eyes

dull feathers full of mites
watch it fly back

to the poplar and its silver leaves
to its nest too thin for the wind

[summer snuck into fall again]

summer snuck into fall again
spat its humid lust
gave the fields brown rain
I am trying to be a different girl
I need the silence here
how it wraps around white stars
builds into the sky a hollow cone
the night has lost its voice
and cannot answer

What Girls Learn

Mama was two women: one who never
spoke on a date from fourteen to eighteen,
one who kicked off her shoes, ran to the stage
and danced with the band until nobody
had anything left. Everything from mashed
potato to the twist, even sexless
chaperones couldn't say a bad word
about her. Because she was that good.
I knew her behind a vacuum, running
from calories, lusting after Lays,
hot pink tube top, earrings big as cars.
I knew her when she didn't want to talk
about it, whatever it was, when she
pretended we did in fact talk about
it, and I had forgotten. Silence like
another person in the house, stealth
and grit inside a red plaid flannel robe,
waist cinched. I knew her when she'd get mad
and Daddy'd try to take her seriously
and fail. I think I learned something about
men and women. I think it wasn't good.

Quick Magic

One grandmother danced with her purse when the men pooped out.
Another scared me with tales of murder:
girls decapitated in convertibles,
blonde hair caked red.

One transformed into white butterflies,
elegant companions for a lonely child,
quick magic in summer.

Another told me about the house where the daughter
cut up her mother with gardening shears,
silver flashes in sunlight.

One filled the faded spots of Oriental rugs with magic markers,
old ladies on their hands and knees,
sherry.

Another lost her daddy in a logging accident,
lost her husband on Halloween,
lost her second in his prime,
lost her mind.

Playboy

I brought popcorn, not enough butter
(ever the anorexic) to my brother
and his friends, found them pored over Playboy,
Madonna edition. In the pantry,
Mama's leftover birthday cake (white, chocolate
frosting) hidden. One discovered it,
mentioned it, and later killed himself
with his father's gun. I couldn't get over
it, *Playboy*, what it had to do with me,
how I was supposed to be taken
seriously. I was supposed to be
taken. One morning a ripped-out page
in the front yard: two women kissing
strawberries off their nipples. My father
told me models went to bed with empty
stomachs. They learned how to live with hunger.

Put Yourself Out There

Our breath trapped in childhood, grotesque monument to decay, to limp string beans,
overripe honeysuckle, over-
sexual Delta soil so fecund
popcorn grows.

They brought us legwarmers, hustle, dawn
like a pale sneer. Algebra took
our temperature, found us un-
responsive.

We could have been determined colds slabs
of disappointment, lardy runners
on red track dust, poisoned by flashbulbs,
by desire.

Put yourself out there, our mamas said,
pink sponge rollers and dead baby flesh.
Disturb pancake makeup, grin shiny red,
grin anyway.

We had thimbles, calculators, now-
and-laters, rain on vegetables, demon
speed, pocket sponges, Swatch watches, chocolate lust.

Our heads, kingdoms in air, gray matter,
real estate, dust of teachers' pets, dreams
Coke-soaked hummingbird cake.

Each year found us clawing further, warships full of teddy grahams. Daddies slipped
us peanut M&Ms in church. Mamas
pinched our fat.

In eighth grade I saw my brother's face change
overnight into a boy, kicking us
out of childhood.

You Can't Outrun the Girl inside Your Head

You are sudden, spoiled
an insistent cold rain
a C student demanding As
all hat and no cattle: hook
line and sinker, paint
the town, cry black tears
you're a girl in a rented convertible
flimsy plastic tiara
on your dyed southern head
Miss Okra 1998
your neck don't match your face
you say "base," not "foundation"
you think everything looks better
in glitter
you have bad skin and a fake tan
scratch too hard, your arm flakes off
like brown confetti
you are pigeon-toed in DTM
(dyed-to-match)
somebody's idea of a prom dress
not mine
you are last year, you are has-been
you're in the bathroom having a meltdown
you're a rumor all over high school
something people use
to make themselves feel better
to make sure you can't see her:
dumb girl in the mirror
in the mirror a dumb girl

First Grade

We ran past the meadow
day followed day into another
I fell in love with her Santa Claus coat
out past the field with the electric generator
we jimmied under barbed wire to cross it
sudden warning of a thunderstorm it was
November when we found it
a house that must've burned down years before
everything on the ground black around it
rubber doll with a hellbent face
chain in the backyard where the dog used to sit

Mute

The night we broke up he asked me to tell
him everything I found wrong with him,
everything that needed to be changed.
I was sixteen, mute as cheese, I told him
you go first.

You have noticeable lips, he said,
a normal nose, and pretty eyes. You care
too much about what people think. You're not
much of a conversationalist. You
don't know how to dress for your body.

We stepped through my window into white moon.
Mama slept down the hall, away from
Daddy for a summer while she worked
on her master's, took courses with teachers
who hated to read.

I didn't live there anymore, but I'd gone
back for that boy, one I'd loved since I was nine
for no reason. In the field in the middle
of the night we made love in the dirt
away from the lights of the town.

There were the stars, restless, appalled.
He'd given me his watch and I wore it
until he asked me the next morning,
Do you plan on giving that back?

Scars

Bumped up tracks
redder than the rest of you.
Rivers of corduroy worn like scarves.
Your little hurts.

Inside: sleek, unblemished.
Inside: the same you God stitched
together—hastily, in Heaven,
then threw down like a stone.

Ruined Ghazal

only a girl gets ruined
prom dress soaked

updo down. hideous
ruin, head full of murder.

bones under skin already in ruin
starved thin, blood without oxygen

heart beating only from habit
red ruin

boys make their way by ruin
snake-like belts, hooded eyes, chapped

fingers finding skin
girls' ruin lies in others' hands

behold this ruin—frosted with rage
riddled with ugly, baked too long in the sun

wet ruins down her face
dumb girl in a dress racked

with ruin. who is she fooling?
all roads lead to ruin

she made her way by ruin
[that girl] sought her ruin in a thousand ways.

Wanted

On the runway of the mostly abandoned airport
planes like surprises overhead
an inhuman Houston August
before she's off to be a freshman
in a state you've never been
you won't want her then
you don't want her now
but you will take her, this girl,
thinner than your type
flatter than your type
plainer than your type
you are twenty with a baby
you still live at home
your mama is religious and disappointed
she dyes her hair red and loves this new one
this girl who will be what she thinks is wanted
summer is a slow dream turning
away, rotting on the sills
a soft apple gone weak with bites
but you will take her anyway
all the bruises mush inside your mouth
all the sweet juice sticky on your chin
you won't want her then
you don't want her now
but you will take her

In the Fog

There is a girl at the window of the burned house.
Her mother is an arsonist,
her father a vulture
with his inky feathers and elegant flight.
Nobody guessed she'd set her own house on fire,
lose a baby inside that way,
tiny body in the fog.
You don't see her during the day
but at night she dances in water on the lawn,
twitch of the sprinkler, thunderous hum
of cicadas. Not vulture,
buzzard,
flying above her,
circling what is and is not home.

Dirty Laundry

Monday: laundry on the line, hug
of sun when clouds move
this barely-80 July day.
Your mother hates me
but won't admit it to herself.
It is the domain of mothers, to study
and to pity. I dip
the long bones of your pants
in wind, clip them to green wire
and think of Christmas
in your brother's house, one added
onto after your parents moved in.
Five years ago we arrived
on our dream three acres and your parents
fled a predatory lender to your brother's house.
I know the place of boundary.
I know how far blood travels.
I know what happens when it leaves home.

Practice

It's the stupid things like returning
from the store to find a husband, sock
on gingham kitchen chair pad, full
of self-hatred, icing his knee. "I know
what it is." He'd stepped off the ladder, shoe
pinched, pivoted to a meniscus tear.
He'd already snapped both ACLs. Good Lord,
we'd been building an awning for sheep. Sheep!
Three neutered miniature boys. Pets. We'd lost
our minds.

It's the stupid things like wearing a hat
driving, blocking the peripheral,
smashing into a doe on the way
to school, ruining the one car Husband
could drive pre-surgery, the one car
I could drive, period, unschooled
on the stick which is just a perfect
metaphor for everything.

It's the stupid things like spaying
a mama sheepdog during estrus,
beautiful Ebe bleeding out
on the operating table, her un-
trained baby, Otis, barking while I howl,
phone on the back porch, Husband stumbling
across the yard. Now we had a puppy
and three lambs, a puppy who chased,
played like puppies do, not Maremmas,
bred as guardians for thousands of years.
But guardians must be taught.

It's the stupid things like learning
Otis will die at less than a year,
congenital kidney failure, this big
gorgeous man named for the Motown legend,
thumping his tail when the vet arrives
with his poison. Elsa replaced Ebe,
Enzo replaced Otis, only sheepdogs
regress on new farms with stupid people
who don't know what they're doing. Saturday:
Leonard bleeding above his eye, Enzo
on his back. Our plan: neuter him. Listen,
it's a different story with three-year-old balls.
It wasn't pretty. It wasn't linear.
What I'm saying is it wasn't overnight.
But you don't get stupid overnight.
You don't get unstupid overnight.
You just get a lot of practice.

The Note

We all fall apart. This
is what I mean to say. And
this: a caress most
peculiar, an adventure
without end. Something
imagined and not lived.
Like our relationship.
Forgive me—
outside, the yellow undersides
of leaves dance as if called.
Who am I to want more than I have?
You don't thrill me anymore. This
is only a whisper now. Tomorrow:
maybe a louder one.
Why on your pillow?
If it bothers you, move
to another room.
I will be lonely in that room too.

Still April and No Spring

Now in the country of lost dogs, smashed cats
Deer baked flat on the side of the road
Brittle last grass of winter
Husks of brown
Brown days and brown shoes and felt-tip pens and worry
Spring is a season of indomitable rage
If you're young
If you feel young
If you feel sure you will feel young again
Now on the ribbon of black tar
Dazzle of bright orange warnings
Before the abandon of Easter's tease
Before the sweet pained trill of a house finch
Whose sweetness makes you sad
And how little those birds are
In the yard in the air in the trees in the rafters
Of the back porch
With their insistent optimism
With their industry and might

Temporary

roads cut into farms here
rip skunks fresh
hurl orange tabbies
I drive to work in tears
allergic to optimism
so when I meet it—
oily red complexion of a colleague
I am my most negative self
temporary, my officemate and me
three years renewed
three years in which nothing has been said
not even his wife's first name
we toss clichés, grin
at the smudged walls behind our heads
I try to find the Southern girl inside
fake sugar
we live on a highway
on acreage we couldn't afford
farther from the road
spring brings Harleys
and their murder
warm weather cooks my brain
classrooms of flesh
bare shoulders, hairy shins
deep furrows of cleavage
it's April
it's temporary
sex drives of the young
one who's scrubbed
her face clean when for weeks
she's made it sparkly
padded bra, white teeth

heart broke
stupid boys
stupid girls
stupid temporary instructor
holding forth
spring brings bodies
out to thaw
what winter bloated
and hid
greets us now
in stench
roars past us
in black smoke

In the Classroom Is a Body

All the boys in the freshman classroom
with their history of longboards
and wild shoulder curls,
pale skin in startled contrast
to the girls, who after break
turn deeper shades of nut brown.
All the boys in the freshman classroom,
videogames with Glocks and piles of bodies,
in the classroom the teacher is a body
rolling on the balls of its feet,
wearing a bra in secret.
The presentation of a body
with its bright optimism and its slow decay,
how the teacher, too, sees a body
for what it is, what it can do, what it won't.

Odes in Juvenile Prison

No first names: it's military prison. Takes weeks
to figure out when the shirt's un-
tucked, there's a child inside. Today
we're writing odes, celebrating
the ordinary. I've taken away gang
colors, replaced
them with Ticonderoga. *Adore*
is a word I have to define, take
out of its box, break
open like a muffin.
It's time to praise something, pretend
there's a whole house waiting
to claim her,
a whole house sitting
on a cul-de-sac. Her name
on its tongue like song.

All We Know

All we know: he was found curled around two guns in the garage,
    a bullet hole
above his wife's collarbone. On the dresser, two wedding rings
    and a tube of lipstick,
mauve. Mama thought she was the most stylish thing with her crisp
    white button-downs.
She'd taught Mama how to iron: collars first, then sleeves,
    then the body
with all its complications. For women, ruffles and darts and pleats;
    for men,
it just is what it is. It was the eighties. There were legwarmers. Somehow
Mama taught Jane Fonda in the pool, her mother and her mother's
    friends
with their thin white hair, pink patches under sunlight. Every time
    I woke up,
my grandmother was out there, treading water.

And I understood it, the need to move in one place, to keep it under
    wraps, whatever it is.
It is yours if you keep it close. Can you be invisible with secrets?
It was the eighties. Girls wore pancake makeup. I hated everything
    about myself.
The nineties were hardly better. Boarding school in the North
    with a Southern accent thick as tar.
But he was found in the garage, and now my friend's got it in her head
    that her grandfather hired
a hit man, staged it to look like a murder-suicide. I know you never
    know everything,
even if the truth seems to claw at you from the inside. I was there days
    before it happened.
I saw him nearly catatonic in the front yard, pulling weeds
    out by the roots.
But that's memory, isn't it? That's the mind forcing a narrative,
    trying to tell itself something that make sense.

Limits

Around here you're judged by your lawn. People
don't go inside each other's houses. Parties
have port-a-potties, air freshener, Purell.
At the last block party her neighbor held
her hand too long, scraped his fingernail
across a knuckle during Hill Billy Golf,
ingenious Yankee drinking game.
To be a girl is to feel shame, still,
at middle age. Secrets kept
until they mold, swell
up her body. It happened after college:
one leg, then the next
five years later. She did this to herself
like that boy drunk in summer pushing
layers of sheetrock in a dorm
until they pressed him to the wall
for days. There are limits
to circulation, limits to how
you can lure the body and it won't
do what you want, it won't be
what you want. She can't have her back,
that girl in shorts, that girl with the gymnast's
calves, ankles slim as wrists. Her body,
metaphor for what was there all along. Batter
needs time to bloom into cake, heat.
It needs to be beaten.

Additional Acknowledgements

"Wanted." *Exit 7*
"In the Fog." *Lake Effect*
"Dirty Laundry." *San Pedro River Review*
"Practice." *Exit 7*
"The Note." *Third Coast*
"Still April and No Spring." *Sakura Review*
"Temporary." *Cobalt Review*
"In the Classroom is a Body." *Poet Lore*
"Odes in Juvenile Prison." *Another Chicago Magazine*
"All We Know." *The Texas Review*
"Limits." *North Dakota Quarterly*

Anne Dyer Stuart grew up in the Mississippi Delta and graduated from Hollins College. She received her MFA from Columbia University and her PhD from The Center for Writers at the University of Southern Mississippi. She has published widely in literary journals, including *AGNI, Cherry Tree, Third Coast, Louisiana Literature, Raleigh Review,* and *The Texas Review.* Her work won a Henfield Prize, *New South Journal*'s Prose Contest, was anthologized in *Best of the Web,* and nominated for *Best New Poets.* She is Creative Works Editor of *Impost: A Journal of Creative and Critical Work* and teaches in the creative writing program at Bloomsburg University of Pennsylvania. She and her husband, Ted Roggenbuck, have five miniature sheep, two dogs, and four (as of now) cats.

www.ingramcontent.com/pod-product-compliance
Lightning Source LLC
LaVergne TN
LVHW041514070426
835507LV00012B/1572